I0659151

Why Do Christians Break Down ?

Why Do Christians Break Down

William A. Miller

AUGSBURG PUBLISHING HOUSE
Minneapolis, Minnesota

WHY DO CHRISTIANS BREAK DOWN?

Copyright © 1973 Augsburg Publishing House

Library of Congress Catalog Card No. 73-78260

International Standard Book No. 0-8066-1325-4

All rights reserved. No part of this book may be used or reproduced in any manner whatsoever without written permission except in the case of brief quotations embodied in critical articles and reviews. For information address Augsburg Publishing House, 426 South Fifth Street, Minneapolis, Minnesota 55415.

Manufactured in the United States of America

Contents

To Marilyn

Preface

This is a book about breakdown. It is a book about that strange and undesirable condition of the human being in which he is simply not able to "hold himself together" enough to make it through the ordinary requirements of everyday living. That in itself is bad enough; but sometimes it is a condition which is only the beginning of something much more severe.

Emotional breakdown can happen to any human being. It can happen for obvious reasons or for obscure reasons. But whether clear or clouded the reasons underlying emotional breakdown are many and varied. For instance, the stress of specific experiences in life (loss, failure, betrayal), the stress of one's job, the expectations of spouse, conflict in the family, unrealistic goals, the demands and pressures of culture and society in general, shifting moral values, nationalistic background, the rapidity of change, the teaching and influence of the church—any of these factors may bring about or contribute to emotional breakdown in a human being.

11

Ordinarily one does not see "the church" included in a listing of possible factors contributing to emotional breakdown. While much has been said and written about the relationship between the church and mental health, and between the spiritual life and the emotional life of human beings, there appears to have been little open discussion about how the church may actually be contributing to emotional breakdown in the lives of some of the people it touches. There seems, even, to have developed a tradition of sorts which suggests that people of faith (specifically Christian faith) do *not* break down.

But Christians *do* break down, and spiritual faith does *not* guarantee immunity. That is statistically verifiable. Furthermore, over the years of my parish and institutional ministry, it has become increasingly clear to me that there *are* specific areas of teaching and influence in which the church may actually contribute to the emotional ill-health and breakdown of some of its members. This is not to say that there is a deliberate or even conscious effort in the church to sabotage man's emotional health, but rather that through certain emphases, traditions, and interpretations the church provides input which may adversely affect the emotional lives of people, either causing emotional breakdown or aggravating a condition which was leading to breakdown.

My purpose in this book is to identify and examine some of those areas of teaching and influence where it appears that the church may be contributing to breakdown. Furthermore it is my purpose to speak to possible changes, shifts in emphasis, and re-evaluation which may be helpful in allowing the power and strength of the church to work for emotional health and total wholeness in its members.

Why do I break down?

I break down because there has been some substantial malfunctioning in my experience of love, and I am not well enough prepared to withstand the stressful situations of life.

1

No Immunity

Anyone who knew her as she was growing up in Wellington, Iowa, could tell you that Adele Carroll was a quiet and shy child. She never smiled much; she didn't even talk much. And it was plain to see that she was insecure and was probably lacking experiences of affection and love. As she herself reminisces about those days, she is quite sure that there *must* have been good times and joy in her childhood at home; but she cannot recall those things.

Adele was the first of three daughters born to her parents—persons whom she describes as stoic, hard-nosed people of German stock, who never really showed any affection. She remembers this especially because affection *was* important to her. She wanted it. She wanted to see it. The Carroll family went to Sunday school and church every Sunday because her father had been reared a strict Methodist and her mother a very strict Lutheran, and on Sunday you

went to church because you should. In church Adele
heard about affection and caring and love. And her
mother and father said amen to it. But she never
saw it. And she wanted to see it.

Her father was a quiet man. He worked hard and
she felt close to him. She liked her father—not so
much because he was a likable person, but because he
in his quietness, was refreshingly different from her
mother.

"My mother," she says, "was an angry, controlling
woman. She seemed to live in a destructive attitude
—one that killed joy and hope and forgiveness. She
wanted perfection. She criticized me continually; I
could never please her. She would put me in a double
bind so that I couldn't possibly do a thing right. I
mean, she would say, 'Love me,' and then when I
would move to get close to her she would push me
away and wouldn't *let* me love her. And then she
would make me feel guilty because I didn't love her.
I felt like a worm all the time I was growing up."

The Carrolls were *both* insecure people. They wor-
ried a lot, they fought a lot, and they managed to
maintain a constant air of tension in the household.

One morning Mr. Carroll decided he'd had enough.
He took a gun and killed himself. Adele, age twelve,
saw him do it.

This was a real trauma for Adele, but her mother
chose not to talk with her about it. Rather she avoid-
ed helping her work through her grief. After all,

grief was useless—there was never anything to be gained by crying. But Adele wanted to cry—and started crying the day before her father's funeral. Good friends and neighbors, however, told her that she shouldn't cry—she should "be brave for your mother's sake."

If she had been generally quiet and shy before, now, going through the four years of high school, she pulled into herself all the more. "I was like a zombie all through high school," she says. "It was a nightmare, and I was often sick to my stomach. Still, I was determined to make it through—and I did. But I was getting deeper and deeper into emotional trouble all the time."

Sometime after graduation from high school Adele pulled together the strength to move out from home and enrolled in a three-month electronics school in Omaha. She liked the course and felt good about the experience—but this only served to push her into a slump of depression. Through her experience of life, Adele had learned to accept the normal as abnormal, and the abnormal as normal. If she felt good, that was wrong. She had to make herself feel guilty or bad or worthless in order to feel right. If she experienced relaxation and calm, she couldn't stand it— there had to be stress and tension. That was the norm for her.

When she finished the electronics course she was so depressed she couldn't take a job, but instead went home (back to the "normal" atmosphere) for three months to "recover." She then went back to the electronics school for a one-month course, and after that took a job in Ohio, working with teletype. She was able to work at that job for six months before anxiety and depression made her quit and move back home.

This was her pattern for the next few years. She was in and out of jobs—she simply couldn't function adequately for any length of time. In the meantime her mother and sisters moved to Minneapolis and shortly after that, she and a sister moved to California.

Adele worked for a while after arriving in California and then got back into school to study music. Unconsciously she sought out a teacher who was very much like her mother, and all the stresses of home were resurrected and given new life. Adele pulled into herself more and more—she became progressively isolated, more dependent, couldn't think for herself, couldn't decide. She moved in with a couple who were her friends; and on a day in May, 1953, Adele Carroll broke down.

She recalls that she was "totally and completely out of it. I wouldn't get out of bed, I couldn't talk, I had spells where I couldn't breathe. I was deathly afraid that I was going to die and go to hell. I literally *smelled* the fires of hell. I had an almost constant image of the crucifixion in my mind which was, to me, my absolute sinfulness. I felt there was no hope."

Adele's mother went to California, and after some

time and some persuading was able to bring her back to Minneapolis for treatment. Even then, she resisted because she was so afraid—of people, of herself, of everything. It was frightening to go into the hospital, but it was a beginning. It was the beginning of the long way back to health.

People *do* break down. People break down every day. *Many* people break down every day. Beautiful women and plain Janes; yellow men and white men; little girls and old ladies; corporation presidents and laborers; Swedes and Italians; Sunday school teachers and exotic dancers; geniuses and low I.Q.s; marrieds and singles; red heads and bald heads; Ph.D.s and sixth grade dropouts; clergymen and bartenders. . . .

It happens! On the average, one out of every ten persons breaks down. So that if you have in your acquaintance one hundred various persons, chances are that ten of them have experienced emotional breakdown. Next time you are in a heterogeneous crowd of two hundred people chances are that twenty of those persons there have experienced emotional breakdown serious enough to require some kind of professional attention. Breakdown happens! It is no respecter of persons!

To break down is not a sin. To break down is not a crime. To break down is not a cause for shame. If I told you I have high blood pressure you would not label that a sin. If I told you there was a dysfunction in my gallbladder you would not accuse me of a crime. If I told you my breast was tumorous you would not look at me in shame.

People who experience breakdown experience *mental* illness. There is something wrong with them— and the "something" is that their overall behavior is not normal or usual. It may be out of touch with things as they really are—and it persists that way. The abnormal, unusual behavior doesn't just happen and then cease. It persists; and the person experiences emotional breakdown.

But why? Why do people break down? Don't they have enough backbone? Don't they have enough faith? Are they constitutionally degenerate? The debate over the question of why people experience emotional breakdown and mental illness will probably continue forever. But until an absolute answer is uncovered, there is abundant research to show that people break down emotionally because at the root of it all there has been some substantial malfunctioning in their experience of love, and they are not well enough prepared to withstand the stressful situations of life. Stressful situations are precipitating factors in mental breakdown and they are indeed many and varied, probably as numerous as there are persons who break down. Sometimes these pressures come from inside a person, sometimes from outside him, sometimes from both without and within.

From within come the pressures to perform, to

achieve, to fulfill expectations, to strive for perfection, to suppress feelings, to deny our undesirable selves— in short, to fulfill our ideal. Add to that the internal pressure of worry, fear, self-doubt, low self-image, the need to please and be accepted.

There are outside pressures also to perform, to achieve, to succeed, in short, to fulfill an ideal; only here it is someone else's ideal. Then, too, there are the stressful situations of disappointment, failure, betrayal, the demands made by others, external conflict, a variety of loss, sickness, accident, misfortune, shame.

Perhaps another way to consider this matter of the pressures and stresses is to perceive the basic forces at work on any one of us at any time in our lives. Consider, for instance, these four:

(1) What I believe I *ought* to be.

(2) What others *expect* me to be ("others" being mother, father, spouse, employer, God, Rotary Club, my best friend, the pastor, etc.).

(3) What I myself *want* to be.

(4) What I, in fact, *am*.

I suppose it would be possible that in a given person each one of these elements could be identical with every other one, and there would be no differences between them which would have to be dealt with. However, for the vast majority of human beings, such is *not* the case. There may, in fact, be large differences between those elements—they may be in conflict with each other—and the conflict generated by those differences may produce tension and stress which may lead to mental breakdown.

Diagramatically, it might look like this:

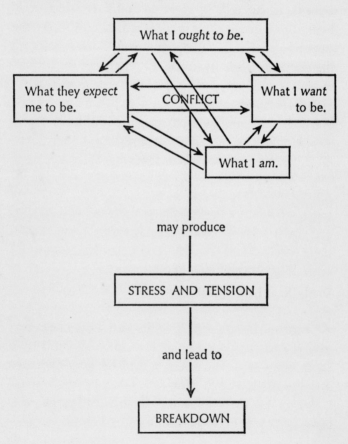

Probably no one experiences all of these possible pressures simultaneously (who could?), and yet things do seem to have a way of piling up. It's like the old adage, "When it rains, it pours." Even before one stressful situation is resolved another has pushed its way in. And then another. And another. They seem to gang up and jump out like muggers from an alleyway.

When the experience of everyday living gets to be too much for the human personality to cope with, it breaks down. The emotional stress and strain is just greater than the person's ability to adjust to it—and the person's ability to function becomes impaired. There is a kind of mental and physical exhaustion, an emotional collapse, which may be classified as mild, moderate, or severe. In a mild breakdown the person may become "weepy," feel excessively tired and tense, lose confidence in himself, be moody, lose his appetite, and have trouble sleeping. In moderate breakdown these same symptoms are present but to a more intense degree and the person is partially disabled in meeting the everyday responsibilities of living. In severe breakdown the person is unable to function; he is severely if not totally disabled. He is preoccupied with his symptoms, his hands tremble, he feels trapped, he doubts that there is any way out, and he may entertain thoughts of suicide.

This kind of behavior is called *neurotic*. The neurotic person maintains contact with reality, but that contact is confused and inaccurate. He perceives reality not as it is but as he is *afraid* it is, or as he wishes it were.

A similar but more severe type of behavior is called *psychotic*. The psychotic person becomes so irrational and unrealistic that he appears to be out of touch with the real world and has moved, either partially or completely, into a world of his own.

Persons who are breaking down often get lots of advice from well-meaning people. The advice may come in phrases like, "Why don't you snap out of it?" or, "What you need is more faith!" or, "Pull yourself together!" or, "What you ought to do is trust God more!" or, "Why don't you stop this foolishness?"

Such advice is more destructive than helpful. In most cases the person breaking down cannot help doing what he is doing, nor can he simply stop doing it when told to. It is like going up to an asthmatic and telling him to stop wheezing on command. Such "advice" can do little more than make the person feel more helpless than he already is. Trying to argue him out of his neurosis will only generate more stress and probably make him defensive. And using phrases like "What you need is more faith" will do little more than induce guilt, making the person feel even less good about himself than he already does, and causing him to feel that even the Almighty is walking out on him.

Sincere, conscious acceptance of a Christian belief

does not necessarily guarantee sound mental health or the cure of mental ill-health. Do not be surprised if someone whom you know to be religious breaks down. There is nothing magical about Christianity which somehow immunizes "the believer" from the tragedy of breakdown. It is risky business to equate Christianity with mental health, for we continue to encounter seemingly "irreligious" people who are quite healthy emotionally. And there is not some kind of qualitative or quantitative difference between believing and *really* believing, so that one could say, "Well, if she *really* believed, she wouldn't break down." Simply saying "I believe" does not exempt anyone from the stresses and tensions of life.

Likewise, the presence of mental ill-health does not necessarily mean the absence of Christian faith and belief. It is truly an enlightened age that we live in— an educated, sophisticated, and liberated age. And yet in many ways we are still caught up in the milieu of old stereotypes, old mores and old superstitions. We believe there is something sinister about mental ill-health and we somehow fear people who have broken down and are neurotic or psychotic. And in that fear we project onto them all sorts of things like weakness, degeneracy, and "unbelief," not realizing that, as the famous saying says, "There but for the grace of God, go I."

The literature in the field of mental health is enormous; there are literally hundreds of facets to this broad subject about which people have written. One facet that has received considerable attention is the relationship between religion and mental health.

In my own experience in ministering to people in crisis, stress, tension, and neurosis—people who have experienced breakdown—I have found that there is very often more than just a coincidental connection between a person's spiritual life or religious experience and his emotional condition. Sometimes it has seemed that some aspect of the person's spiritual life was the precipitating factor in his breakdown—that it provided the stress that the person became unable to cope with. And so I began to raise the questions: Could it be that religion (the church) has occasionally contributed to the mental ill-health of people? Has the church at times been guilty of some basic offenses against mankind that produce stress and tension within people? Has the church forbidden man to affirm his humanity? In other words, has the church allowed a person to be human? Or has it expected him to be superhuman, while telling him that he is sub-human?

My own professional experience was corroborated through conversations with other professionals who have dealt with thousands of persons in breakdown—counselors, psychiatrists, clergymen, psychiatric nurses, social workers, and psychologists. The observation was especially borne out by the many people who had themselves experienced breakdown and recovered, and could affirm that in their experiences the church had played a major role in their breakdown (and in many cases, in their recovery).

On the basis of my investigation I came to this observation; it has seemed to me that the church has contributed directly or indirectly to the emotional ill-health and breakdown of many of the people it has touched.

I realize that that is a broad generalization and as soon as I state it I make myself vulnerable to a variety of challenges. For instance, someone is sure to ask, "What do you mean by the church?" And the biggest question is, *"How,* specifically, has this happened?"

To try to speak to the question of what I mean by "the church" is admittedly difficult. For one thing I do *not* mean any specific congregation or denomination, or one's home church or any specific movement or person. I am thinking more of something admittedly very nebulous—of the traditional, organized, structured, established church; of the teaching and preaching of the church through some of its clergy and laity —the seminaries, the dogma, the tracts, the church school literature, mottos, devotional literature, hymns, verses.

Let me try to come at this with another question: What does a woman mean when she says to me, "I learned in church that it is wrong to be angry?" What does she really mean by "in church"? Possibly she picked this up in sermons, in private conversation with clergy or laity, church school teacher, a catechetical

help, a Bible commentary, a tract, devotional literature, a sermon theme on a church bulletin board, a
hymn, her parents, who were "religious" people. What
she means by "in church" probably she herself is not
even sure. But she associates this with "the church."

I am aware that many persons will honestly deny
that their experience in the church is anything like
the description in my generalized thesis. And a good
thing! But this simply points up the shortcomings of
any generalization—the exceptions. The thrust of this
book is to hold up the shortcomings of the church
which *do* in fact contribute to breakdown and to try
to speak to them and hopefully move toward allevi-
ating them. That not all congregations, clergy, teachers, literature, and pious parents will manifest these
shortcomings is axiomatic.

Specifically, how has the church contributed to
breakdown? The following chapters seek to give an
answer to this question, but let me present here a brief
overview of the areas that raise concerns.

1. There seems to have been a kind of doctrine in
the church which says that if a person really has faith,
he will have no fears or doubts or concerns or questions; and conversely, if he *has* any of these things he
does not have faith. There seems to be a panacea titled,
"What you need is more faith!" (This is part of the
"if—then" syndrome; *if* you believe, *then* such-and-
such will take place.)

2. There seems to have been in the church a tendency to stifle the expression of real, personal feelings (for instance anger, ecstasy, despair, grief) and to encourage a consistent "neutral pleasantness" as the proper way to express oneself.

3. There seems to have been in the church a tendency to stress a kind of false personal security and goodness by denying and repressing the dark sides of human personality.

4. Largely through legalism and authoritarianism there have been oppressive demands made by the church in terms of behavioral expectations; and phrases such as "you must," "you should" and "you ought" have helped create burdens which have weighed heavily on people.

5. The church seems to have had a tendency to paint much of life as either black or white with little consideration for the specific situation.

6. The church has seemed to stress the worthlessness of man, seemingly encouraging people to be ashamed of themselves almost to the exclusion of being proud of themselves. There has appeared a preoccupation with reminding people of how bad they are, and a fostering of a kind of false humility.

7. While declaring him to be truly human, the church

has played down the humanity of Christ and has presented an image of Jesus which has appeared to be superhuman. For a person to try to identify with Jesus as the church has so often presented him makes for extreme frustration.

Sometimes these things come through explicitly, sometimes implicitly. Sometimes they are mixed into the general philosophy of "pious" parents and grandparents. Sometimes subtly, sometimes blatantly they have been implanted into receptive consciences. I have seen too many people whose lives have been impaired in varying degrees by a church which seemed often to be oppressive. And that distresses me. I do not believe it is healthy simply to condemn an "oppressive church," but I do believe that it *is* particularly healthy to hold up in public view what seem to be specific shortcomings and to speak to possible changes or solutions.

Why do I break down?

I break down because I cannot allow myself to express or act on the very real feelings, and especially negative feelings, which I experience within myself.

2

Real Feelings

Many of us are afraid of our feelings—those inner experiences—the height and breadth and depth of our inner reactions to people and events. To many of us feelings are strange creatures and we don't really know what to do with them or, worse yet, what they will do with us. There is a whole host of feelings we may experience, running the gamut from almost total despair to almost absolute ecstasy. All of which turns out to be quite frightening because it seems that our feelings are seldom under our control. There seems to be a definite line between the rational and the irrational here; we experience feelings but we seem to have no rational control over them. That may be scary, or at least embarrassing, and so we tend to think that maybe we ought not have feelings at all, or at least we certainly ought not express them openly. After all, mature people should be in control of themselves. And we have come to believe that if you go around expressing your feelings openly, you are certainly not in control of yourself and you are not behaving as a mature adult.

For instance, if you experience the feeling of anger within yourself and you openly express that anger verbally, many people will tell you that you are lacking in self-control and that you ought to "cool it." If you feel sadness and grief and you openly express that feeling by crying, you are exhibiting a lack of self-control (or worse if you are a male) and someone will inevitably tell you to "pull yourself together." If you feel joy and exultation within yourself and you openly express that by dancing or jumping up and down or shouting gleefully, you have lost control of yourself and someone is sure to tell you to "settle down." If you feel the inner pain of depression or fear and you manifest your feeling and verbalize it, you are out of control of yourself and someone will remind you to "keep your chin up, it's not all that bad."

All of these behaviors are appropriate and acceptable for children. For mature adults they are inappropriate and unacceptable—thus the "helpful" but suppressive responses from other people, such as "cool it," and "pull yourself together." When we become adults we are supposed to have put aside such childish behaviors. The unfortunate thing is that to become adult *this way* may be very costly—the price may be emotional breakdown.

Where did we ever get this idea anyway? Where

did we ever get the idea that being mature means that you are always in control of yourself and therefore do not show your feelings? Where did we ever get the idea that to express your feelings is inappropriate, undesirable, possibly unchristian and certainly indicative of weakness and insecurity?

These ideas come to us from our culture and society *in general*. We get this indoctrination from home, school, church, and business. And the result is one of the major problems contributing to the confusion, anxiety, and ultimate breakdown of American people: the inability or refusal (either conscious or unconscious) to experience or express one's feeling reactions to people and events. People lock in and bury their feelings so extensively that counselors and therapists spend most of their time and energy trying to help such troubled people uncover and unlock their true feelings to find a foundation for establishing a new balance in their lives.

Many of us begin to learn early in life that it is desirable to put the lid on the expression of our feelings. Male children are still told, "Big boys don't cry." Little girls play with dolls and only rarely are seen pushing a toy bulldozer aggressively through a dirt pile. And of course we learn by observing our parents as we're growing up. If they do not express their feelings, and if we want to emulate them (as do most children) this will add substantially to the tendency to push down the expression of our feelings. There are those, too, who believe that national origin or geography influences the expression of feelings or lack of it. For instance, Scandinavians are generally observed to be "cold" and quite unexpressive of feelings, whereas Latin Americans are said to be "hot" and very openly expressive of feelings.

Thayer Greene in his excellent book, *Modern Man in Search of Manhood,* recalls: "I had both the fortune and misfortune to be raised in the psychological ethos of New England where the capacity for spontaneous feeling expression and response is not exactly encouraged. New England Congregationalists, from whom I stem, have been all too accurately characterized as 'God's frozen people.' For the sense of structure and roots provided by such a Puritan ancestry I shall always be grateful. But finding the capacity to reveal and express spontaneous feeling would be easier for someone raised in Rome or Vienna or in a Negro or Puerto Rican home. The white, middle-class Protestant generally has the greatest amount of peeling to do if he really wants to get in touch with his feeling side." I would agree wholeheartedly with Greene, but would hasten to add to his last observation that white, middle-class Catholics are generally not much better off.

Home, school, community, business, that is, society and culture in general do indeed contribute substantially to the suppression and repression of feelings in people. And the church has been no exception to this generalization. The church has not helped make it easier for people to be openly expressive of their feelings. In fact, if anything, the church seems to have been busy stifling feelings, telling Christians implicitly that it is more desirable not to express feelings, and sometimes even, not to have the feelings at all.

The church in its very structure and worship has traditionally fostered the suppression of feelings. If there is any one word which seems to characterize the traditional Christian church it is "solemnity." The church is solemn. The worship is solemn. So the people must be solemn. There are more things that you just don't do in church; there are more things that are inappropriate in church than anywhere else. Quiet prevails; seriousness is the mood; liturgy and hymns are generally done "with reverence." Traditionally the sacrament of holy communion has been "celebrated" in great solemnity, and at least as often as not, an air of near gloom has surrounded it rather than an atmosphere of celebration. It is inappropriate to truly rejoice in sacred settings. The church has seemed to filter itself through propriety and formality.

Now I am certainly aware that there are glowing exceptions to this assessment. The most obvious, of course, is the "gospel" church which throughout its existence has been celebratory and openly expressive of feelings. However, for the more "sophisticated" church this kind of behavior has been traditionally unacceptable and inappropriate, not "respectable," perhaps even of a lower caliber.

In a very quiet way the church seems to be saying, "It is desirable to be steady, reserved, quiet, 'unemotional.' The Christian life is better exemplified by a consistently level, bland, neutral, pleasant, 'nice guy' pattern of behavior."

When it comes to certain specific feelings, however, the church seems to be much more explicit. Fears and anxiety, for instance, appear to be feelings whose expression is not welcomed in the Christian person. Christian people tend to deny and put down authentic feelings of fear and anxiety because the expression of those feelings may very well be interpreted as lack of faith. On the one hand, they may hold this position themselves, demanding of themselves the putting aside of such feelings, believing that it *is* lack of faith to feel and express fear and anxiety. Or on the other hand they may want to express those feelings, but instead suppress them, believing that if they do express them, others (family, friends, fellow church-members) will judge them as being of little faith and will say something like, "There now, you *do* trust God, don't you? Why the fear? Yea, though I walk through the valley. . . ." This seems to be especially true of people who are in adversity, people who are suffering from illness or disease, people who are to undergo treatment or surgery.

A case in point was Mrs. Riordan, a patient in a metropolitan medical center. She had been admitted with the diagnosis of a very serious disease. After five

weeks of intense effort, her doctor informed her there
was nothing more he could do for her diseased condition. He was kind but honest. She might not live more
than six months; then again she might live for fifteen
years.

She felt a wave of anxiety sweep over her when she
heard his words. She felt a flush of warmth all over,
both inside and outside. She knew her eyes were filling
up and she could feel her throat becoming dry. She
heard him say that she could be discharged from the
hospital in a day or two; and then she saw him leave
the room.

That afternoon the chaplain stopped by to visit her.
He had talked with her before, so they were not strangers. She had told him of her religious background
and something of her family and much of her hopes
and expectations for recovery. He was aware of what
her doctor had told her and he wanted to minister to
whatever needs she might manifest, especially in view
of that distressing announcement.

He found her teary-eyed, but she managed a slight
smile as they greeted each other. She told him almost
immediately about her doctor's report and he tried to
respond by picking up her apparent feeling of sadness
and disappointment. She seemed to want to discount
that with a pleasant kind of stoicism. They talked
more and she indicated that she wondered what it
would be like to live knowing that you might die at
any moment. The chaplain tried to respond to her

feelings of anxiety and uncertainty but she rationalized her situation, reminding him and herself that no one at all ever knows when he is going to die, and everyone has to die sometime anyway. When the chaplain tried to empathize with her in her sadness over a shortened life and to help her express her fear of dying she again rationalized and denied her feelings by smiling weakly and saying, "I guess I really should be happy; I've been blessed in many ways."

What was it that prevented this woman from unlocking her obvious feelings of fear and anxiety? What prevented her from expressing them and sharing them with someone who obviously cared? Was the risk too great—the risk of showing her humanity? Would it be too threatening to her to admit to her feelings? Would she be allowed, as an admittedly religious person, to *have* fear and anxiety? Or would that be an indication of weakness of faith and thus cause her to see herself and, perhaps to be seen, as a lesser Christian? Was it necessary for her to deny her authentic feelings in order to meet expectations?

"Christian people bear up under adversity." This is a maxim of the church. It speaks to feelings of fear and anxiety, and it also speaks to the feeling of grief. People experience loss, disappointment, failure, betrayal and they grieve, they get depressed, they despair. Such feelings are natural reactions to the experiences of life, and yet there is a real question as to whether the church allows Christian people to express such feelings.

How often have you heard well-meaning Christian friends say to the bereaved spouse at the casket of her husband, "There now, look up. No need to cry. You trust God, don't you?" With my own ears I have heard clergymen speak these very words to grieving relatives who had just experienced the death of a loved one in the hospital.

How much damage is done when the natural grieving process is thwarted will depend on the emotional strength of the individual himself. But no one is completely unaffected. If either consciously or unconsciously I believe that I must bottle up my natural feelings of grief over a loss and must not express them for fear of appearing to lack faith, I put myself under considerable pressure and make myself liable for breakdown. This is true also of the feelings of fear and anxiety dealt with above.

Often people do not allow others to have and express strong feelings because they themselves are afraid of them. If I, for instance, fear death, I tend to want to avoid dealing with it within myself. So if you begin to deal realistically with death—either your own as you express your fear and anxiety, or perhaps the death of a loved one as you break down and cry—I will be very much threatened and frightened by your openly talking about it and expressing your feelings. When you are not in control you frighten me, and because I am threatened, I will endeavor to make you stop. I will tell you not to be afraid or not to be anxious or to take heart or to have faith—I will give you false reassurance or any kind of meaningless encouragement that I can come up with, because your behavior (your honest openness) is threatening me and I cannot tolerate the uneasiness.

The religious dynamic figures in here quite prominently. If I feel within myself that I must hold to and demonstrate a "perfect faith," I will be on shaky ground and will have to keep reinforcing myself to believe (to kid myself) that my faith *is* perfect and free of doubt. But if I relate to someone who does manifest doubt, questioning, and wavering I will be unable to accept it (because I can't accept it in myself) and I will be heard to say something like, "Oh, don't talk that way!" or "Have more faith and you won't be depressed."

Healthy faith always has its ups and downs, that is reality, and most of us intuitively realize that. However, because of their own insecurity, some people cannot allow the "downs" in others and do in fact destroy healthy faith by condemning (in a "nice" way) the downs. Those persons who happen to be influenced by a person such as this soon begin to suppress and internalize their feelings and begin to present the dishonest facade of never having any "downs." They also, at the same time, begin candidacy for breakdown.

I said earlier that one of the maxims of the church is the statement, "Christian people bear up under adversity." I believe that is possible. I also believe that it is possible for people who are just as Christian to break down under adversity. Therefore, let me accept my brother in his doubt; let me help him express his fear and anxiety; let me allow him rightly or wrongly to have his feelings; and let us look together for the help and strength that very definitely lies in the Christian faith.

One other feeling singled out for special attention in the church is anger. A powerful feeling, anger seems to be the feeling with which Christians have the most trouble. It is the feeling people believe they must stifle more than any other feeling (even sex), and which when repressed or suppressed seems to cause more trouble than any other. A psychiatric nurse once told me that in dealing with patients on a mental health unit for several years, she observed that the majority of patients at any given time were in a condition of breakdown because of unexpressed feelings of anger. She herself, she said, had experienced a breakdown years earlier primarily because of a build-up of unexpressed anger which she directed inwardly and thus created a severe depression within herself that necessitated hospitalization and shock treatments for cure.

This woman grew up in a religious home; in fact her father was a clergyman. She learned early in life —in her home and in her church—that the expression of anger was inappropriate, unacceptable, and certainly not a part of the behavior of a Christian person. So she internalized it. Whenever angry or hostile feelings came on her she repressed or suppressed them because this was expected of her. Through the years she fulfilled that expectation successfully, until one day the price of that success became clear—she broke down. All the bottled-up, unexpressed feelings had taken their toll.

A passage in Scripture says, "Be angry, but do not sin; do not let the sun go down on your anger" (Eph. 4:26). That admonition is an excellent piece of advice for anyone who wants to pursue sound mental health as well as the Christian way. Unfortunately, it seems that the church has tended to mis-read the passage and reports it as saying, "Do not be angry for you will sin." Or, at least, the church has so heavily emphasized the latter part of the passage that it has almost eliminated the first two words.

The mere title of a sermon on a church bulletin board carries teaching power and influence. It "represents" the church. So that anyone who saw the bulletin board which I saw some years ago received quite adequate reinforcement for the notion that anger is wrong. Below the name of the church and the name of the pastor were listed the worship times. Then came the sermon theme for the following Sunday. It was titled, "The Sin of Anger."

It is rather difficult for anyone to live his life totally avoiding conflict and disagreement. Part of the genius of our humanity is our individuality and uniqueness. We are different from each other! And those differ-

ences will cause conflict and disagreement and anger
and hostility. To deny this is dishonest. To deny this
natural part of human life is self-destructive. If there
is any sin involved in the feeling of anger, the sin
must be in the denial of it. Isn't that what Paul is
really saying in that passage from Ephesians? "Don't
let the sun go down on your anger—express it appropriately at the time you feel it—get it out, don't
hang onto it overnight—don't push it down into yourself and carry it around for days or weeks or years—
express angry feelings as they occur, don't let them
pile up one upon another until you break down under
the pressure."

All this holds true not only in our relationships
with our fellow human creatures, but with our Creator
as well. People *do* get mad at God. People are sure
to get mad at God, if God is real to them. But to
express anger to God seems out of place in the church.
"Fear the Lord," is more often heard; or, perhaps,
"You can't talk back to the man upstairs." The church
has seemed to use "the will of God" as a means of
dealing with (suppressing) feelings of anger toward
God. For instance, if I begin to feel within myself that
I have been dealt a dirty deal by God and I begin
to express any of that, the church (religious relative,
friend, or pastor) may say to me, "This is God's will
for you; accept it." That very nicely pushes my feeling of anger underground; and it may get a further
push if someone says, nicely, to me, "If you only had

more faith you wouldn't have to feel angry." That not only adds to my volume of anger, but also encourages me to bottle up all the more my feelings of anger and keep them inside where they can work to break me down.

Then too, I may happily use the "will of God" concept myself to handle my negative feelings toward God if I believe that to feel anger toward God is wrong or sinful. People often do this in times of tragedy, loss, or death. In the midst of their pain they experience great feelings of hostility toward God who is supposed to be in charge of the universe. However, they suppress or repress those unacceptable feelings and employ the acceptable mechanism of rationalization by saying, "It was God's will."

Because anger can be such a strong feeling, people tend to accept all the more readily the concept that anger is wrong or sinful. We so often associate anger with violent behavior and destructive physical acts that we agree with people who maintain that the expression of anger is animalistic. We want to avoid it altogether because we have seen it handled badly or destructively. That is indeed unfortunate because anger is a real feeling in the life of every human being, and it must be dealt with.

Not only that, it is frankly impossible to live without experiencing virtually the whole gamut of feelings. We need to realize that the experience of feelings is natural to the human being. To deny this is to deny our humanity. And yet, that is what the church has sometimes asked people to do. "Keep an even keel, consistently steady, without wavering from a neutral pleasantness. Be passive, don't be assertive. Be sweet, don't be angry. Be modest in celebration. Have faith, don't doubt. Trust, don't grieve."

All feelings have an emotional charge of energy; and no one can dispel that charge simply by denying or repressing the feeling. I mean you do not get rid of the emotional charge of an angry feeling simply by denying that you are angry and smiling pleasantly instead. You only drive the emotional charge underground, and that does no lasting good whatsoever, only harm. I was reminded of this when I read how large companies are disposing of industrial wastes by pumping them into underground wells or abandoned mines. The trouble is that the wastes may pollute underground water systems, or, if forced in under pressure, may simply burst out somewhere else.

The analogy is clear. Repressed feelings can contaminate other systems; they can cause some people to become physically ill. Their physical illness is certainly real, but it is emotionally induced. On the other hand repressed feelings can build up under pressure and finally burst out in mental breakdown.

If a person believes his feelings are wrong to *have,* he will certainly believe they are wrong to express. If, however, he can accept the fact that life is full of situations and experiences and events and people that naturally generate the whole spectrum of feelings within him, he can feel free from guilt in expressing them and no longer need to repress them. He can feel inside that he is *allowed* to fear, allowed to grieve, allowed to rejoice and celebrate, allowed to doubt, allowed to be angry. Many of our feelings are transient, they are not long lasting, deeply imbedded charges. If we can express them the charge is often quickly dispelled. If we repress them consistently we only make for trouble. There is more to be said about the actual healthy expression of feelings, but that is more appropriate to the final chapter.

The possibility of insight into and breaking out of old patterns of denial and repression of feelings is articulately described in the following paragraph, written by a middle-aged male student as he evaluated his experience in a Clinical Pastoral Education program. He said, "I have become aware of some freeing up of unexpressed, frozen feelings in myself, and the feelings of others are becoming to me more readily recognized. This is beginning to help me gain greater confidence to minister to the needs of others. It's been tough to be trapped, and I don't expect rapid change. I have become aware of my dishonest dealing with my feelings at times, putting them down by denial rather than dealing with them. The result has been that my feelings have gone underground making me feel unconsciously destructive towards myself and others. By over-control of my feelings and not allowing room for feelings to be felt in the moment, I have experienced that the buried feelings have only returned later as powerful and dangerous strangers from within to confuse me and speak a confused message to others. But I have become aware of what has been taking place; I have come to insight and now I intend to act on it."

Good luck, in discovering your humanity!

Why do I break down?

I break down because I am afraid to admit that evil, unacceptable, inappropriate tendencies still exist within me, even though I have committed myself to the way of Christ, and I cannot accept them as being truly a part of me.

3

The Shadow

My uncle was an especially gentle man. My aunt and he were responsible for my rearing since my mother and father both died when I was a young boy. Consequently I knew him well, and felt him to be a warm and kind-hearted man who, almost to a fault, put the most charitable construction on virtually everything that anybody ever said or did. Still, he was a jolly man who knew how to laugh and enjoy a good time.

One afternoon, when I was about ten, an incident occurred to my uncle which both amazed and amused me. I really didn't know what to make of it at the time, but it lingered, vivid in my memory, and finally, many years later, I came to realize that on that afternoon I witnessed probably for the first time in my experience, a memorable performance of *the shadow*.

Mrs. Helen Davis, a widow and long time friend of

our little family, came to our house for a visit, to spend the afternoon and evening with us. This was not particularly uncommon, for she had been in our house many times, and we in hers. Mrs. Davis and my aunt had been friends when they were girls and the friendship continued consistently over the years, even after each had married. My uncle liked her, not only because she was a friend of his wife, but because a closeness and fondness had developed between them, too, over the years of their acquaintance.

On this particular afternoon my uncle was home when Mrs. Davis arrived. In fact all three of us, he and my aunt and I, were together in the kitchen when she came to the door. The kitchen always was the most popular room in our house and the kitchen door was the most frequently used entrance. Mrs. Davis came in, and my uncle, as a good host, took her coat, and, as I recall, simply laid it over a chair back. When she took off her coat, she revealed that she was wearing a simple print house-dress, a smock-type that was closed by a zipper that extended the full length from top to bottom of the front of the dress.

I probably would never have remembered that Mrs. Davis even visited us that afternoon, to say nothing of remembering precisely what she was wearing, were it not for what happened the moment after she took off her coat. Some superficial conversation began immediately, but my uncle seemed not to be in it. Rather he simply smiled a little, faced Mrs. Davis directly, placed his left hand on her right shoulder, took hold of the zipper of her dress with his right hand and zipped—straight from under her chin down to the hemline of her dress. He straightened up, took one step back and surveyed his work.

To this day I wish that I could have been able to capture the whole episode on film. There stood Mrs. Davis with her dress hanging wide open, absolute astonishment etched into her face. My aunt stood two feet away in utter disbelief. And I in my childish innocence stood there giggling a little, but wondering too, if perhaps my uncle Lou had lost his mind.

He soon regained his awareness and was feeling obvious shock and remorse. Very seriously he said, "My God, Helen I'm sorry. I really am! *I just don't know what came over me.*"

When Mrs. Davis got herself put back together again we all laughed about the episode and wrote it off as a humorous anecdote, agreeing that it was something we would all remember for a long time. And indeed I did! But not until many years later did I realize that what "came over" my uncle that afternoon was . . . his *shadow.*

One of the most fascinating aspects of the study of human nature is the realization that each of us possesses a shadow or shadow side to ourselves. I say fascinating because it is both exciting and frightening to discover this. To gain any new self-knowledge or awareness of ourselves is always an exciting adventure;

but it is also always a little frightening because we are never really sure what we are going to find, and the unknown inevitably carries with it the aura of danger. This is especially true of coming to know the shadow, the dark side of a human personality; even the words "shadow" and "dark side" are foreboding. And because of this, I believe, not too many people (and especially religious people) are anxious or even willing to look into their shadow sides. To do that may mean that one would have to revise his self-evaluation towards a more realistic appraisal, and who really wants to do that!

What is this shadow?

Something interesting occurs in the process of civilizing the human being. I mean this in terms of "rearing a child." We all know that if children were left to themselves, they would develop as little more than animals. We have seen this in the feral children who have been discovered after having grown up in jungle or wilderness without benefit of human nurture and rearing. Furthermore, any parent also knows that small children who are left to behave "naturally" often appear aggressive, uninhibited, lustful and strongly egocentric—"little devils," as some people call them.

In the process of growing up, each human being, then, is supposed to grow out of, or be educated out of, or be saved from all these undesirable tendencies. As St. Paul said, "When I became a man I put away childish things." We seem to expect this of everyone.

I am afraid, however, that this is the mistake we often make as parents, teachers, pastors—as people in general. We think we have successfully got rid of these inferior, undesirable tendencies, when in fact all that happened is that they have been pushed into the background and stored away in the dark closets of our being, all the while continuing very much alive. Our conformity to what is expected of us leads us to behave in the acceptable way. And much that is rightly a part of the human personality gets pushed away into unconsciousness. This mechanism of forgetting or repressing works so well and is often so successful that many people come to believe that they *are* exactly as they *appear* to be, and that frequently proves to be disastrous.

Every human being *has* a shadow side—a dark counterpart to his bright side. It is the nature of the universe that there be opposites. There is the inferior along with the superior, the undeveloped along with the developed, the unacceptable along with the acceptable, the primitive along with the sophisticated, the awkward along with the coordinated. The shadow is, for instance, the inferior being within ourselves —that part of ourselves that wants to do all the things we would like to do but will not allow ourselves to do; it is the being within us that is everything that we are not. It is a foreign personality—a primitive, uncontrolled, instinctive, animalistic kind of being— the being we dislike because it is so undesirable (lustful, avaricious, conceited, idolatrous). It is the collection of uncivilized desires and feelings that simply are not congruent with social standards or customs or expectations of family, church or job. The shadow is all that we are ashamed of. It is all that we do not want to know about ourselves.

From what I have pointed out thus far, it seems to follow that there should be a very real correlation between the size and intensity of a person's shadow and the style or type of milieu or atmosphere in which he has "become civilized." It seems that the more narrow, rigid, restricted, "closed" and suppressive is the environment in which one develops and lives, the more massive and intense will be his shadow. Likewise, the more open, expressive and accepting the environment, the less massive and intense will be the shadow. Thus, a child reared in legalism and rigid piety is likely to develop a shadow of some substance because of the amount of repression that is needed to meet the requirements of that kind of atmosphere. There are simply more thoughts he is not allowed to have, more words he is not allowed to speak and more behaviors he is not allowed to perform, and these must all be repressed.

The more massive the shadow, the greater the danger of it breaking through its owner's consciousness and causing him trouble. This is simply because there are more behaviors that have been denied and repressed and which have the power sometime, somewhere to come forth and overwhelm the person. Remember, none of that repressed "stuff" just evaporates or withers away.

Maybe this is something of what the nursery rhyme is reflecting when it says:

There was a little girl, who had a little curl,
Right in the middle of her forehead.
And when she was good, she was very, very good.
And when she was bad she was horrid!

To acknowledge my shadow! To realize that I am capable of great evil as well as great good! Well, that may be good theology, but it is much easier and seemingly more desirable instead to deny the shadow and say that the "old man" is dead and properly buried. Then I don't have to deal with the shadow.

Oddly enough, when we see this happening in people and identify it, we can't quite be comfortable with them. We tend to be "up-tight" and cautious around someone who is "just too good to be true"; as if we intuitively realize that true humanity is spiced with wickedness, and, as superstition has it, it is only the *devil* who casts *no* shadow.

It seems that it has been relatively difficult for many people of the church to accept the reality of the shadow and to see it as a valid part of the human being, which must in fact be dealt with. Legalism, authoritarianism, and rigid pietism have helped produce giant shadows in people because of their tendency to deny

the humanity of human beings and to demand repression of earthiness.

Religious people often say that the whole thrust of
Christianity has to do with the death of the old man
and the coming forth of the new person in a rebirth.
If you are reborn you will not think, speak, and behave in ways unbefitting a reborn person. You simply
will put out of your mind any such thoughts or plans.
You will repress and deny the shadow. There is no
room for any of the aspects of the old man (the
shadow side) when you have really committed yourself to Jesus. And if such aspects should continue to
be in your awareness, then you obviously have not
really committed yourself.

Not only is this poor theology, it is also detrimental
to mental health. It is the perpetuation of that old
error of equating Christian commitment with observable action, and stressing behavioral change for its
own sake instead of stressing relationships which
may *result* in behavioral change. It is possible to see
people who exercise tremendous willpower in a
struggle to hold themselves on top of their moral
expectations; people who can confess no weakness
either to themselves or to others. They have not
reached this spiritual level naturally but have erected
by force a rather artificial tower which is constantly
in danger of breakdown under a slight additional
burden. Such people do not seem to be able to get
in touch with their own feelings, they cannot enter

into meaningful relationships, and the more tendencies they repress into their shadows, the more neurotic they become.

It is as useless to deny the shadow as it is to try to repress it completely. The shadow is unavoidable and a person is incomplete without it. Denying it only causes trouble; therefore a person has to find some way of accepting it and living with it. Mental, spiritual, and even physical health may very well depend on this.

What is basically necessary here is the acceptance of a more realistic image of humanity. I mean an emotional kind of acceptance, not just an intellectual acceptance which says, "Well, no one is perfect." We all know that. What is involved here is perhaps the giving up of cherished ideals, albeit ideals which to begin with were unrealistic or based on an illusion. For instance, the ideal that "I *never* allow my eyes to wander lustfully after any member of the opposite sex," or "I *never* allow myself a negative thought about anyone of a minority group," or "I *always* look for the best interpretation of other people's behavior, and *never* have an uncharitable word about others."

Such ideals are unrealistic and illusory. Trying to live as more virtuous than we really are is an effort to deny the reality of the shadow by working diligently to keep it from breaking through. All of which may very well lead to collapse and breakdown. Worse yet, it seems to work in reverse: the more I try to deny my shadow, the more vulnerable I am to its breaking through.

If the situation were right, would it be possible for me to destroy another human being?

Yes.

If the situation were right, would it be possible for me to cheat and steal?

Yes.

Would it be possible for me as a man to take another man's wife and leave my family, or for me as a woman to take another woman's husband and leave my family?

Yes.

Obviously it takes courage for us to admit to possibilities such as these lurking within ourselves, even though we are people of faith—Christians. Yet virtually any daily newspaper will attest to their reality. Therefore, it is somewhat unrealistic *not* to admit to their possibility, hard as it is. Besides, there is real value in knowing and facing such a thing; it can then be dealt with. In the unconscious, nothing changes. For instance, a woman who unconsciously hates her husband so much that she "could kill him" may very well do that very thing in a fit of violent anger; and then afterward say, "I just don't know what came over me." Whereas if she had been aware of these violent feelings and had not repressed them, she would have had the opportunity to deal with them and to try, somehow, to change the situation.

If I am consciously aware of some aspect of my shadow side, I can deal with it. I can accept it. But because I say, "I can accept it," I do not mean that I have to act on it or even give a positive value to it.

Suppose, for example, a clergyman becomes involved in a counseling relationship with an attractive and desirable woman. In the course of the relationship he may experience sexual feelings for the woman. Now, what shall he do about the feelings?

If to admit to having such feelings is morally repugnant to him, he will deny that they exist and will repress them. However, in doing this, he puts himself in danger of "unwittingly" falling in bed with her. He has become ripe for his shadow to break through and empower him to act on his repressed desires. Later he may be heard to say, "I just wasn't myself."

On the other hand, the clergyman who recognizes and admits to such feelings, knowing that having such feelings is not necessarily abnormal, but is a real part of his humanity—such a clergyman can consciously deal with these feelings and is *not at their mercy.* His acceptance of those feelings does *not* mean that he plans to seduce the woman. It means that he acknowledges his feelings, keeps them conscious and honestly determines whether or not they will get in the way of a helping relationship. If he feels they will, he refers her to someone else. If he feels they will not, he continues the relationship.

People foolishly are threatened by admitting to "undesirable" feelings and thoughts, when in fact it is much more dangerous to deny their existence, when their existence is really only normal and natural, and pretend that they are not there. *Then* one is in real danger of being overcome by them—he is no longer master of his own house. It seems that the shadow which is repressed acquires strength in the unconscious so that when the moment comes that it must appear it is often more powerful and more likely to overwhelm the rest of the personality which otherwise might have acted as a governor and prevented the behavior.

I don't believe that I am ready to say that I know precisely what happened with my uncle that memorable day in the kitchen of our home. It just seems to me that here was a repressed desire, which may very well have been pushed down for a long time, into my uncle's shadow side. To see this woman so exposed was a real desire to him, just as it might have been to *any* man. But it was an unacceptable, even repulsive desire, and was consistently relegated to the shadow instead of being accepted and dealt with consciously. Then one day when the setting was right, the shadow of my uncle simply broke through the denial and repression and made him do what no respectable man does. And he never really knew what overcame him.

Why do I break down?

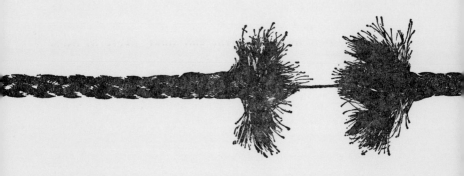

I break down because I feel a need to present myself as something other than I believe I really am, and the pressure to keep up the front and play the role is just too much.

4

False Faces

"Who is Charlie Green?"

And the young man just sits there across from me in my office, somewhat stunned, somewhat puzzled, even though that is his name.

So I repeat the question again, a little more slowly this time: "I said, Who is Charlie Green?"

There is true perplexity on his face now because he is sure I am after something, but he doesn't know what it is. And he wants very much to answer it in a way that will be acceptable to me because it seems to be important to him that he please me.

So in some desperation he says, "I'm not sure I know what you mean; how do you want me to answer that?"

And I reply, "I'm not sure I even *know* how I want you to answer it."

By now he is clearly angry with me and with himself as he feels the very uncomfortable feeling of frustration—all this because I have asked him, "Who is Charlie Green?"

"*I* am Charlie Green," he says finally.

I nod my head and say, "That's good for openers. Now what can you tell me about this guy?"

The frustration hangs on as he says again, "I don't know how to come at it; how do you want me to approach it?"

I shrug and say, "Approach it any way you want. Describe yourself to me in any way you choose. Tell me what you will about who Charlie Green is."

He relaxes some and says, "Well, I am a student . . . I am married . . . I am an American. I was born in Pittsburgh . . . my parents were Irish . . . I'm a Democrat. . . ."

And I sit there saying to myself, "Why can't he tell me who he really is? Why can't he tell me for instance that he is the kind of guy who feels deeply hurt when he sees injustice and apparently can do nothing about it—that he is a man who enjoys poetry —that sometimes he catches himself defending a bigoted position—that he is very much in love with a woman—that on some days his religious faith literally pulsates within him while on others there is an absolute drought? Why, when I give him the unrestricted opportunity to describe himself to me in any way he wants, why does he choose to describe himself to me in terms of *roles?*"

In 1969, John Powell wrote a little book titled,

Why Am I Afraid to Tell You Who I Am? Early in the book he answered the question of the title by quoting a person who had said, "I am afraid to tell you who I am, because, if I tell you who I am, you may not like who I am, and it's all that I have." Powell goes on to say that in order for a person to be truly human and fully functioning he must overcome that fear and let other people discover who he really is by allowing his external or exterior life to reflect accurately what he is feeling inside.

From the approach of Powell's statement it would seem that human beings very often lead "double lives"—the outside being different from the inside; or perhaps we could say, public life being different from private life. And indeed we *do* lead double lives, or triple or quadruple. Not that we are all necessarily schizophrenic personalities, but that as we live our lives we do play different "parts" or roles very much like actresses and actors who play roles in a drama. We put on and wear different masks that befit the roles we are playing, again very much like those actresses and actors of the ancient stage.

The reasoning behind this behavior seems to rest on our need to conform to what is expected of us— to please others and thus feel accepted by them. However, because of our human individuality, the behavior expected of us by society (others) may not be the behavior we would rather perform. We people are very much like a winding stream as we proceed through our development. We want to follow the path of least resistance and develop in the way that is easiest for us. Therefore there is this inevitable bind: on the one hand we want to "go our own way," and yet on the other we want to look good and acceptable, or, as we say, "put our best foot forward." The result is that in the process of maturing there is a compromise which takes place in every one of us—a compromise between what we are and what our society expects us to be. And this compromise becomes the mask through which we relate to the world outside ourselves.

Edwin Arlington Robinson describes this phenomenon quite beautifully, I believe, in his short narrative poem, "Richard Cory." Here you see a person who apparently played his role exquisitely, right to the end.

Whenever Richard Cory went down town,
We people on the pavement looked at him:
He was a gentleman from sole to crown,
Clean favored, and imperially slim.

And he was always quietly arrayed,
And he was always human when he talked;
But still he fluttered pulses when he said,
"Good morning," and he glittered when he walked.

And he was rich—yes, richer than a king—
And admirably schooled in every grace;
In fine, we thought that he was everything
To make us wish that we were in his place.

So on we worked, and waited for the light,
And went without the meat, and cursed the bread;
And Richard Cory, one calm summer night,
Went home and put a bullet through his head.

A much less dramatic but more common illustra-
tion of relating through the mask is found in our manner of responding to the simple question, "How are
you?" You are walking down the hall, or through the
plant or pushing a cart in the supermarket and someone you know appears and says, "Hi! How are you?"
Do you respond out of your true self or through a
mask? Let's say it has been a rough week; things have
not gone well at all. There has been a mild crisis in
your family and you have been nagged by a common
cold. To answer out of your true self would necessitate
sharing some of those feelings with the person who
asked you how you were. You might say, "Well, not
really very good today," or "It's been a rough week
and I'm feeling pretty low." Chances are, however,
that you will instead respond through your mask and
smilingly say, "I'm fine, thank you. How are you?"

We in our society seem to feel that it is expected
of us to be in control and on top of things at all times
—that it is desirable always to be pleasant and cheerful. Because we do not particularly like to hear other
people's complaints ourselves, we rationalize and say,
"I do not have the time to tell her how I really am,"
or, "She really doesn't want to know how I really

am." Besides, if you respond honestly to her question you believe that she will probably think less of you, and mentally brand you a complainer, even though she might smile politely through *her* mask and say to you, "Oh, I'm sorry to hear that."

Because we tend to be so sensitive to what we feel is expected of us we seem to be almost continually picking up signals describing *how* we should conform to our role. These signals come from home and family, the church, the employer, friends, "the image makers" in advertising, television, magazine articles, and books, to mention some of the more obvious sources. Those sources which we for one reason or another admire, respect and value are of course more influential and impressive than others. For instance, the signals given to me by my employer concerning how I should play my vocational role will carry a lot more weight for me than will a magazine article. However, for another person the exact opposite may be true.

Now when it comes to vocational calling we see the wearing of masks and the playing of roles most clearly, and we see people very much concerned about adopting the characteristics expected of them in the vocation they have chosen. For instance, the business executive must play the role of the energetic, driving, creative person because this is the way he is stereotyped. The scientist should be comparatively cold and impersonal, dedicated and self-sacrificing. The drill instructor must come on tough and authoritarian. Educators must be intelligent. Persons in finance should be conservative. Nurses must be compassionate without getting involved with their patients. Salespeople should be aggressive without forgetting that "the customer is always right." Taxi-drivers and bartenders must be quasi-analysts. Barbers and beauticians must be conversive and witty. Politicians should always be right. Clergymen should be pious. Waitresses should move fast. Religious educators should always have an answer.

It is certainly true that when we take up a vocation we all adopt to a certain extent those characteristics which are expected of us in that vocation. We know this, and we know too, that it is quite necessary to do so in order to succeed. Furthermore, it is also true that people choose vocations for which they feel best fitted. However, the *role* is never the *whole* woman or the *whole* man; there is much more to her and to him than that. And not only that, human beings simply are not consistent, even though role-playing demands consistency. Consequently there is an inevitable falsification that must go on in a person when he plays a role and wears a mask. Let me try to illustrate.

I said that according to society's expectations, one who plays the role of educator must be intelligent. Of course she must! Who wants a dummy for a teacher! But to what *extent* and how consistently must she appear intelligent? Must she consistently provide an answer for every question that is put to her? Must she be an expert on all matters of academics? Can she never make a "stupid mistake?" Will she feel tremendous loss of face if she were ever forced to say, "I don't know" and *could* she even say it? Does she seem to be "teaching" continually? Is she compelled to "keep up the image" at any cost?

Or consider the salesman. He is supposed to be the "hail-fellow-well-met" type; aggressive, confident, and understanding of his customers. He hadn't better be despondent—even if he *is;* that's not good for sales. He must be consistently tolerant and accepting, even when he cannot stomach the treatment he receives from some of his customers. What shall he do with feelings of inadequacy and personal doubts—sell his family and even himself on a pollyanna future? "Next month is going to be great!" Do people say of him: "That guy is *always* selling"?

A person's spiritual life gets very much tied up in wearing masks and playing roles too, for it seems that we are generously provided with descriptions of the true spiritual life and expectations of the role of the Christian.

The church has not been lax in telling people how they ought to live—how to think, how to feel, how to speak, how to react, how to dress, how to work, how to use leisure, what to look at, what not to look at. In our present generation there is even a revival of this legalistic structuring of the role of the Christian. This again is an indication of what seems to be the church's stress on equating spiritual life with observable behaviors instead of equating it with relationship. To do this is reasonable, though, because it is much easier to define a role in terms of what a person does and what a person does not do, than it is to define it in terms of a relationship which produces behavior.

Let me stress that masks and roles are necessary. Through these we relate to our world. In a positive and perhaps protective way masks and roles shut off a person from his natural, instinctive life—the mask may tend to prevent the shadow from breaking through. People who never really develop masks or play roles are generally gauche, ungraceful, "bull-in-a-china-shop" types who do not have a feel for propriety. Masks and roles actually facilitate our relationships with other people because they indicate what we may expect from them—they help make us more predictable.

The very real danger of it all lies in the possibility of identifying oneself so strongly with the role he is playing that he begins to believe that he really *is* what he appears to be. You get into trouble when you cannot distinguish your real self from your mask, and you say to the world, "I am my mask; I am only a role; I am always a role." For many, role-playing is so deeply a part of us that it is virtually the only way we have of identifying ourselves. When I asked that young man sitting across from me in my office, "Who is Charlie Green?" his primary way of identifying himself was in terms of roles and images or masks (occupation, national background). And he is certainly not unique. In fact, he is typical. I think this phenomenon is borne out even in the matter of simple introductions. I am impressed how consistently people use roles to identify the persons they are introducing. "Harry Brown, I'd like to introduce you to Sam Jones. Sam, Harry is a stockbroker with Smith and O'Brien. Harry, Sam is a graduate student at the university, working on a degree in geology." Or, "Louise, I'd like you to meet Harriet Olson; she's the wife of Doctor Olson and also the chairwoman of the Village Charity Antique Auction this year."

There is indeed a strong tendency to identify with one's role. There seems to be something very appealing, even seductive, about office and title and degree. "I am the foreman of the line." "I am the pastor of the church." "I am the teacher." "I am the president." On the basis of this, some persons are little more than the distinction or pretentiousness given to them by society. And it is difficult indeed to find a personality behind their shell.

If my basic identity is my role I will continually relate stereotypically of that role. But I may find myself in serious trouble if a critical situation presents itself—one which might demand flexibility on my part, or perhaps an entirely new way of relating, entirely different from the way of my mask. I may break down and fall apart because I am unable to cope with the situation in the typical way of my role, but I am also unable to adjust in order to react in another way because I am too locked into my role. For instance, if I typically relate out of a smiling, cheerful, "everything-will-work-out-fine" kind of role, I may very well find myself totally unable to cope with a situation that demands my tearful empathizing with someone who is walking through the valley of despair and needs me to walk with her.

So there is a real possibility of trouble when you cannot distinguish your self from your mask. There is also danger in a loosely-fitting mask or role. I mean, the possibility of trouble is directly related to the discrepancy between the role and the true self. The larger the difference between the mask and the true personality, the greater the possibility of trouble. Of course if the role does not fit at all, life is unbearable.

Think of the son who is persuaded to follow his banker-father into "the business." He is a liberal, free-thinking person whose artistic talent is strong, and he is much more of a feeling-type than a thinking-type person. To live the role expected of him in the appropriately conservative atmosphere of the bank imposes tremendous stress on the young man and will inevitably drive him to breakdown if he tries to wear such a mask which is so radically opposite his true personality.

Or consider the woman whose husband was an office clerk with "the company" when they married. Over the years he "worked his way up" until he finally became a vice president. And along with his climb came accompanying expectations of her as hostess. entertainer, socializer. But she is by nature a reserved and introvertive type of person, much more desirous of intimate relationships in small numbers than the superficiality of big parties. She prefers the quiet and the natural to the noisy and the showy. But it is *expected* of her and she must pretend. The question is of course, how long she can keep up the pretense before it becomes unbearable and she breaks down.

Still another source for possible trouble is the need for *consistency* in playing a role. Here the words "always" and "never" play such a big part, where morality and spirituality figure strongly and where the church has had a big input.

Again, it is basically the issue of whether one is able truly to accept his humanity or not. Am I a person who loses his temper occasionally and behaves irrationally? If I can accept that I am, then I don't need to deny it by putting on a mask of placidity, pretending that I am always calm, rational, and in control.

Am I a person who sometimes gets to feeling so overwhelmed by things that I would like to say, "To hell with it all"? If I can accept that I am, I don't need to deny it by putting on a mask of serene assurance, pretending that I am always confident and have the feeling of being "sufficient in the Lord."

Am I a person who can feel my natural sexuality become aroused by an attractive member of the opposite sex? If I can accept that I am, I don't need to deny it by putting on a mask of prudishness, pretending that I never have a sexual thought and pretending to see nothing which I ought not look at.

Am I a person who can admit to the coming and going of doubts and questions and dry spells in my faith and trust? If I can accept that I am, I don't have to wear the mask of pious certitude—pretending always to be solid, strong, and courageous.

"It gets pretty hard to keep up the front." I hear that from many, many role-players. But people often feel compelled to keep it up *consistently,* and they will not allow themselves to *be* themselves and so they *do* keep up the pretense until they break down. And break down they do. When you consider the number of role expectations that are made of most of us, it is not too difficult to realize the pressure and the strain that leads to breakdown. For instance, there are expectations of marriage, role expectations that each spouse has for the other. What kind of part are you expected to play as a wife or a husband? There are expectations of family, of parenthood. What kind of mask do you wear as parent? I have already dealt with the huge role of vocational calling. There are expectations of your role in your community. What mask do you wear there? In your church? What mask there? And on and on.

Somewhere, sometime, a man has to become his own man and a woman her own woman. No one can everlastingly be all things to all people—and not break down. Let me know myself in my strengths and weaknesses, and accept myself as I am. Let me wear my masks and play my roles, but all the while knowing that they *are* masks and roles, and it is *I* that am I. Let my outer self be congruent with my inner self and let me have no fear of presenting myself just as I am.

Why do I break down?

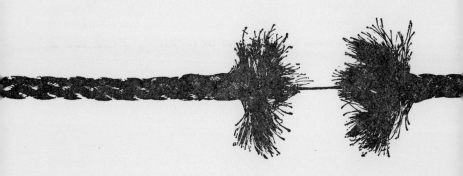

I break down because I cannot allow myself to think highly of myself, and as my self image deteriorates, I despise myself more and more until I can no longer see worth or value in myself.

5

Self Image

I had known Joan as a nursing student for about a year and a half. From time to time we had sat down together and talked, mostly about her expectations, problems she was having with her identity, and about relationships with young men, and one young man in particular. One day as we talked, she told me that she was in trouble academically and she was very much concerned about it. The problem seemed to be that she was so preoccupied with the issues of her emotional life that she seemed to be just about on the borderline of being able to function adequately in fulfilling her day-to-day responsibilities. This turn of events did not at all help what seemed to be emerging as her primary concern, namely, "Who am I?"

Joan reported that she had a very low image of herself and, as far as she could remember, had "always" felt inferior. She had to "do" things to gain attention, and it seemed that what little positive image she had of herself was almost entirely dependent on others' affirmation of her. She had grown up in the church, and she knew that it was simply not right to think too highly of yourself; people do not like people who "inflate" themselves.

Then an event occurred which seemed to give her problem a new dimension of seriousness by shooting her self-confidence and self-image to an all-time low. She had spent the previous weekend at home with her parents. Friends of the family had been invited for Sunday dinner. Everything had been quite comfortable until after dinner Joan's mother suggested that she play a selection on the piano which was sort of a favorite of that particular group. Joan tried to shy away gracefully, because she was afraid to play— afraid she would come off looking her "usual rotten self." But her mother insisted, reminding her that she had even won first prize in a contest once, playing that particular selection. Joan knew that too, she said, but it didn't help give her any more self-confidence. Finally she reluctantly sat down at the piano to begin the selection, and then it happened. She felt a wave of fear, she felt hot, her mind was a total blank, she could not find even the first chord. She broke down crying, ran out of the room, upstairs to the bathroom and vomited.

She was miserable as she recounted the episode to me. As we sat together she proceeded to put herself down in virtually every facet of her being, describing how truly worthless she was. Finally I said to her quietly, "Joan; are you ugly?"

She looked a little surprised, but answered, "Well, I think I'm fat."

"Are you ugly?" I asked.

"Well I could at least stand to lose a few pounds off my hips."

"Are you ugly?"

Her response came a little slower now. "I *do* have this mark here on my face."

But before she had finished her sentence I got up and took her by the arm over to the clothes closet in my office. Inside the closet there is a mirror. I opened the sliding door and positioned her directly in front of the mirror and said to her one more time, "Are you ugly?"

She looked silently. There was a long pause. She turned slowly to me and with a faint trace of a smile she said firmly, "No; I am not ugly."

We both sat down again. "Are you stupid?" I asked.

"Well, there certainly are a lot of other kids who are a lot brighter. . . ."

I broke in. "Are you stupid?"

With a little frown she replied, "My I.Q. isn't that great."

"Are you stupid?"

"No. I am not stupid!"

"Are you obnoxious?" I asked immediately.

She started to laugh. "Alright, alright," she said.

And it was clear to me that she had begun to come to insight.

It was only a beginning, of course. But we worked together trying to reconstruct an image that was realistic, a self image that recognized its pluses as well as its minuses, a self fit to live with, and to feel good about.

Joan did not break down. She was pretty close, but she managed to step off the downward spiral of self-devaluation before she went into a serious depression. But how many others have been unable to make that step off the spiral! How many others have repeatedly and consistently put themselves down and *felt* put down until there seemed to be no end to the spiral, and they broke down, unable to cope with everyday life!

Self image, or how a person views himself, is extremely important in the development and maintenance of emotional health. If I have learned to have a poor and lowly image of myself I will tend to be self-depreciating, insecure, lacking in confidence and self-assurance, full of doubt and fear. I will expect to be rebuffed, or ignored, or hurt in the relationships and experiences of life; I will expect to be put down because I put myself down. I will have no pride in myself as a person, I will degrade my accomplishments, I will be shamed by compliments, I will reject praise and thanks from others.

How a person could develop such a low self image

is readily seen in the situations where parents continually tell their child that he can't do anything right and will never amount to anything at all; where he is constantly scolded and criticized and his achievements are ignored or put down. That is to say he is *worthless*.

We can rightly lay much responsibility on the home for generating such poor self images in children, who carry those images along with them into life, either breaking down ultimately or else living a sort of half-a-life existence. But has the church any responsibility in this? Has the church fostered a self-depreciating stance in Christian people and held up lowliness as an ideal? Has the church encouraged people to be ashamed of themselves almost to the exclusion of being proud of themselves? Has there been a preoccupation with reminding people of how bad they are? Has there been a fostering of a kind of false humility?

In the church I attend we have evening worship services in the homes of members during the Lenten season. The worship is quite informal. We sit around on the floor or in chairs, generally fourteen or so adults and maybe half as many children. One night I was attending a service with a group about that size, and somewhere in the midst of the pastor's very informal sermon he asked us where we believed we ranked in the "talents received" column. He had been talking about Jesus' parable of the talents and wondered if we saw ourselves as one-talent, five-talent or ten-talent people. He asked for a show of hands. "First of all," he said, "how many of you believe you are ten-talent people?"

I raised my hand and then I looked around and realized I was the only one in the group with my hand raised. As I remember, I think he eased his hand up then too, and sort of smiled at me and I at him. We exchanged a few words, and then he asked how many believed they were five-talent people. Still no hands went up. Finally he asked how many believed they were one-talent people, and a few hands were raised. Some in the group never raised their hands at all.

It was obvious that the question made the people in the group feel very uneasy. They really didn't know what to do with it. And so we had something to talk about together for the remainder of the sermon time.

The disturbing thing is: why should a question like that make Christian people feel uneasy? Why shouldn't Christian people be able to answer it straight forwardly, affirming themselves? It seemed that there was evidence here of a kind of tension within Christian people—a tension between what they feel themselves to be (or at least definitely *want* to feel themselves to be) and what they believe they *ought* to feel themselves to be. The "ought," I believe, is the product of the teaching of the church.

I mean, I knew many of the people in that group to be talented and gifted and to possess a variety of abilities. And they knew it too. When we talked about it together, some of them expressed their reluctance to identify themselves as having many abilities for fear of boasting—for fear of being considered a braggart. They had learned that you "just don't do that." That would be pride, and we learn from a variety of sources, but especially in the church, that pride is a deadly sin. You should put down pride. So there was within many of those people a real tension—a sort of intuitive self-affirmation ("I *know* I am blessed with abilities") on the one hand, and on the other a fear to express that self-affirmation ("No one likes a proud person").

Granted, there is nothing quite as obnoxious as arrogance. The flagrant display of pride is loathsome. We instinctively seem to detest the egotist. There is no question but what this kind of behavior is undesirable; it is not the kind of behavior that God designed us for. This kind of behavior lacks love for fellows and love for God. It is clear that the church should speak to this behavior and hold up its destructiveness and encourage Christians to avoid it.

It seems, however, that in speaking against arrogant pride, the church has swung the pendulum almost completely to the other side and has encouraged Christians to feel worthless. In the fear of appearing too proud, the church has stressed the goal of lowliness. The *emphasis* has been on thinking lowly of oneself. This is manifest both overtly and covertly. The traditional hymns of the church seem to lean much more heavily in the direction of low self-esteem than in the direction of positive self-affirmation. Words like "my wretchedness and blindness," and "my vileness" stand out glaringly. In one of the traditionally popular hymns the hymn-writer states that one of the two greatest wonders of life is "my own worthlessness." Another old favorite of the church used to wonder how Jesus could ever die "for such a worm as I."

Contrary to some opinions, this "worm theology" of Christianity has not yet experienced metamorphosis. It is still alive. It appears not only in hymnology but in liturgical forms of the church and is particularly evident in confessional prayers. It is instilled early in youngsters by diligent Sunday school teachers and reinforced by parents who believe the same because *they* were taught the same thing. Parents who are particularly hostile and legalistic have much ammunition at hand to shoot down their children's self images, all in the name of Christianity.

Poor self image is not an occasional thing! There are many exercises employed in growth groups to stimulate participants to self awareness and sensitivity to others. One such exercise is to ask each person in the group to write on a piece of paper three positive things about himself as a person, and three negative things. It has been my experience in dealing with church groups that Christian people have, without exception, quickly completed the column of negatives, but had at least some, if not considerable difficulty listing three positives.

Another exercise is to ask each person in the group to talk about himself for three minutes saying only positive things, such as listing positive attributes, talents, accomplishments, achievements, etc. Again, in my experience of dealing with Christian people, the majority of persons quit before the three minutes had been used up; or if they went the full three minutes, there were many long pauses of silence in between their sentences.

I am afraid that many of us in the church have looked much too lightly on this whole matter. The destructive quality of self-defamation is quite sufficient to lead to breakdown. It is crippling. A person gets depressed. He despairs. He comes to *believe* that he is nothing and can do nothing. He is incapacitated —not overnight, but gradually. He not only puts himself down, he despises himself—he hates himself. His self-value and self-worth may become zero—worthless.

Sometimes I am led to believe that it is demonic for a Christian person to consider himself or to believe that he should consider himself as worthless. When Christians do this it must satisfy the great Adversary to no end. For a human being who knows himself to be, as a human being, the highest and finest of God's creations on this earth—for a human being to know this and yet to assess himself as something less than human—to literally or figuratively prostrate himself face down in verbal mire, all the while believing he is pleasing his God, must be demonic. And the prince of devils must indeed be pleased to no end when it happens.

There is a very striking interchange between the priest and the psychiatrist in William Blatty's fascinating novel, *The Exorcist.* It is near the end of the account, and the two men have paused in the labor of exorcising the young girl. As they talk, Damien, the psychiatrist-priest, says to Merrin the exorcising priest, " 'Then what would be the *purpose* of possession? . . . What's the point?' "

" 'Who can know?' answered Merrin. 'Who can really hope to know?' He thought for a moment. And then probingly continued: 'Yet I think the demon's target is not the possessed; it is us . . . the observers . . . every person in this house. And I think—I think the point is to make us despair; to reject our own humanity, Damien; to see ourselves as ultimately bestial; as ultimately vile and putrescent; without dignity; ugly; unworthy. And there lies the heart of it, perhaps: in unworthiness.' "

One of the Latin phrases from theology says: "Simul justus et peccator." Roughly translated it means: "At one and the same time justified and sinner" and it refers to the Christian. Personally, that phrase has meant a lot to me as I have sought to come to grips with my human condition and accept it. It helps me to feel that I belong, that I am justified by God, even though I fumble and stumble and fall short of what I believe are his wishes for me. I am yet a man of real value, of inestimable worth. I am proud to be me!

To keep the two—*justus* and *peccator*—in reasonable balance is desirable. To overstress one is easy, but destructive. And this, it seems, is what has happened too often in the church. *Peccator* has been stressed so strongly that *justus* has almost gotten lost. Though there certainly exists an explicit teaching of the gospel in the church, there also exists an implicit (maybe even explicit) fostering of low self image as a desirable goal for Christian people. And as long as people are encouraged to think more lowly of themselves than they ought, breakdown will continue to be very real.

Why do I break down?

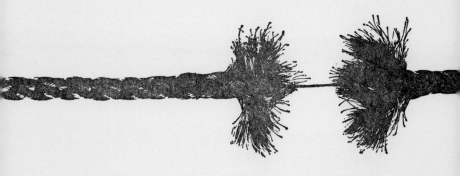

I break down because I try to fashion
my living after Jesus' example when
that example appears to be superhuman, lacking in the basic facets of
humanity with which I can identify.

6

Jesus

There must be no one in the history of the earth
who is known to more people than is the man, Jesus
of Nazareth. And in view of the fact that mankind
has had such precious little factual data about him, this
observation is staggering. Furthermore, we are told
that there has been more written about Jesus than
about any other person in history. And this is all the
more staggering since again the primary resource
information available about him amounts to just a
few ancient manuscripts which only lightly sketch a
very brief (less than one-tenth) portion of the man's
life.

Certainly from all this it ought to be obvious that
there is something very special about the man, Jesus
of Nazareth. And it will do no good to write off that
simple observation as blatant naivete—it is too important. Great mysteries surround Jesus. This fascination
with him throughout the centuries *must* speak to these

mysteries. Very often when people come to know all about something they tend to lose interest in it, and move on to something else. But Jesus has held the attention of people for almost two millenia. The mystery is still there.

The biggest part of the mystery, of course, is who he is. From those sketchy accounts in the collection called the Bible it is said that in Jesus, God did indeed become a man. Jesus himself is reported to have said he and "the Father" were one and the same, and whoever had seen him had seen "the Father."

That great mystery about Jesus seems to have upset people right from the start—and rightly so. If this is true, Jesus is unique. And having no prior experience of such a phenomenon, men set out to try to deal with it. Oddly enough, as fascinating as mystery is, there is a drive within people to solve mysteries and to be able to explain them rather than simply to accept them as mysteries. That is both fortunate and unfortunate. In the case with Jesus, it is unfortunate.

Among the followers of Jesus a variety of explanations were offered to try to solve the mystery of Jesus' identity. Some were accepted, some were tolerated, some were denounced as heretical by the early church. In time the conclusion reached by the church was that Jesus was indeed truly and fully God *as well as* truly and fully man; or, to put it another way, Jesus was truly and fully divine *as well as* truly and fully human.

That should have settled it; but obviously it didn't. Because all that did was to define the mystery all the more sharply. This creedal statement (which we still confess in the church) needed to be accepted as a mystery rather than understood as an explanation which itself would in turn have to be explained, interpreted, decoded. But accepted as a mystery it could not be.

Where and when the arbitrary distinction between "sacred" and "secular" came into being, I do not know. But come it did. And it seemed to work very neatly into the problem of who Jesus is.

By those standards, Jesus was sacred; obviously. Sacred implied goodness, righteousness, purity, and holiness; whereas secular implied worldliness, the mundane, earthiness, the "lesser" at least. (These stereotypical connotations seem to be everlasting.) Being sacred, Jesus would be sacred in his divinity and in his humanity and one could neatly view his humanity as sacred. You just would not *think* of Jesus' humanity as being secular.

But maybe that's not it at all. Maybe that's only a rationalization. Maybe it's simply that people were and always have been afraid just to accept Jesus' true humanity. Maybe it was too threatening to their faith and trust in him. If he were truly a man like other men, what makes him any different from other men? Oh yes, of course he is truly God, but as truly man he *must* be different as a man from other men, else how can people believe he is truly God, and stake their lives on him?

A great many years ago there was a heresy in the early Christian church called docetism. This heresy seemed to stem from some people's inability to perceive how anything material (tangible) could be anything but evil. They firmly believed in the imperfection of matter (tangible things). On the other hand they believed that that which was of the spirit could only be good, high, and desirable. Furthermore they believed there was constant conflict between the two. For there to be any kind of real union between that which was spiritual and that which was material, or between that which was infinite and that which was finite, was totally impossible.

The application of this belief to the person of Jesus caused the docetists to see him only as spiritual and not as real. They said it was only possible for him to *seem* to be a human being; he was not in reality a human being. He was not a real or natural person; he was more a phantom of sorts. Thus, though he seemed to be a man, he only *appeared* that way, and was, in fact, not a human being at all.

Sometimes, as I have considered the image and the form in which Jesus has been presented by the church, I have been inclined to wonder if this heresy of docetism ever really died, or whether it doesn't live on, quietly, subtly but strongly influencing our perception of Jesus. In the traditional presentation of the person of Jesus his divinity and humanity have been (verbally) equally affirmed; but the edge has been taken off his humanity in the actual portrayal of him. In his humanity Jesus comes off as superhuman or as dehumanized. From some descriptions of him, I am convinced that he must have walked around, continually six inches above the ground, and couldn't possibly have known what life was at all about because he was totally above or outside of the feelings, the passions, the experiences of human beings.

Why do we as a church seemingly have to defend or protect him from his own humanity? Is it because we have difficulty accepting ours? If not, then why the need to see him, whom we confess to be truly human—why the need to see him as above or outside of the typically human characteristics? Why should it be so difficult to perceive any kind of earthliness in Jesus? Why should it be difficult to see Jesus as cross and irritable after a hot and demanding day, in need of tenderness and acceptance and refreshment? Why should it be hard to perceive that Jesus could belch gas after a hearty slug of wine? Why should it be shocking to realize that Jesus made mistakes, misjudged, doubted, lost his "cool," threw back his head and laughed loudly, ran into temptations at virtually every bend in the road? Why should we have the need to immunize him from so many of the host of feelings that human beings experience? As a church we seem to have attempted to keep Jesus in a kind of greenhouse, protected and safe. We should probably either *affirm* his true and total humanity, or else quit *confessing* it.

Much of the negative reaction to the rock opera, *Jesus Christ, Superstar* seems to have come out of feelings of fear because an image has been threatened. Understandably so. To many persons, new artists pose a threat to the conceptions of Jesus which old artists have drawn. But what seems to be a threat could, in fact, become a great benefit. It could begin to present a real person with whom people truly can identify— a person who has lived a human life, feeling all the feelings of a truly human life. To be able to begin to perceive Jesus as a genuine person could remove much of the stress of trying to emulate a superman.

This has been, perhaps, the most damaging aspect of this whole matter of the person of Jesus. Christian people know very well the injunction, "Imitate Christ!" But what kind of image has the church traditionally set up for Christians to emulate? An impossible one? One which has only the positive aspects of human behavior, and ignores or sweeps aside or explains away the negative aspects like weakness, short temper, disappointment, resentment, and a whole host of others that all of us are familiar with but which we traditionally *never* associate with Jesus.

Trying to imitate the traditional stereotypes of Jesus makes for real conflict in the human person; and people break down because of the stress and pressure of trying to get off a superhuman performance while in the midst of it all being reminded how worthless they are. It is an impossible task to imitate Jesus as a superman when you are only a man—that is, without breaking down. It is an impossible task to emulate Jesus to the denial of your own humanity—that is, without breaking down.

But doesn't that somehow make him "lesser" than he should be if people perceive him in his true humanity, if people perceive him as being other than sweet and serious virtually all the time? No! What really makes him "lesser than he should be" is to deny him the fact of having lived an authentically human existence.

But doesn't even he himself speak of perfection? Doesn't he tell us to "be perfect," as the Father in heaven is perfect?" Yes! And he is speaking about wholeness and completeness. That is what the word translated as "perfect" literally means. Jesus admonishes us to strive for completeness as persons, to strive to become whole beings, integrated, sound, healthy. To accept our humanity in its fulness as he accepted his is the goal to which he directs us.

What makes it possible for us to accept our humanity is the fact of God's acceptance of us as we are. Jesus appears as the embodiment of God's love and grace; if you want to know what God is like, you look at Jesus. And when you see Jesus walking through the gospels you see and you feel the love and acceptance of God. You see in him your reconciliation with God and you are free to live a truly human life.

To imitate Christ is an impossible task, *or else* it is a healthy admonition, depending upon your image of Jesus. He presents us with a "way." He is the "way." He gives himself to us and shows us how to walk the way. He encourages us to walk it. He promises to walk it with us.

What to Do

"Among all my patients in the second
half of life . . . every one of them fell
ill because he had lost what the living
religions of every age have given their
followers, and none of them has been
really healed who did not regain his
religious outlook."

—CARL GUSTAV JUNG

7

What to Do

Adele Carroll moved easily in her chair. We had been talking together for quite some time. She appeared to be a little tired, and yet she was eager to share with me as much as she could about her breakdown. She had been telling me her feelings about how the church had affected her emotional life in so many ways, both directly and indirectly. She told me how as a child she felt the heaviness of the law—the stress on the commandments—especially the one which demands so much of the child without seeming to lay any corresponding responsibilities on the parents. She had great difficulty respecting and loving her parents, but she felt she had to, regardless. When she couldn't, she felt guilty and condemned. There was a feeling of no forgiveness, of rejection by God.

Even gospel became law: "You *must* love!" it said. She tried, but failed, and only experienced more guilt. She began to lose her sense of self-worth; she began to hate herself. She kept hearing about love in church, but she remembered having no opportunity to feel it, to experience it through human relationships. Instead she recalled the church to be dogmatic, ritualistic, lacking in warmth and "preachy."

Somewhere in the midst of all this I asked her, "Why, in the face of all this, didn't you just pull out and abandon the church?" "Because," she said, "for some reason I believed that the church was the agent through which good would come to me. *I believed that God's faithfulness would prevail.*"

Adele continued to describe to me her painful experiences. She pointed out clearly, but with no malice, how the church had perhaps unwittingly but very definitely helped her along her way towards breakdown. "But," she said, "even though the church failed me terribly, it nevertheless provided me with that one spark, that has been mighty strong, to pull me through as a child and an adult to where I am now." And then she said, "The very thing that contributed immensely to my breakdown, *was also the element that helped immensely in my restoration!*"

What to do?

Adele Carroll and many others like her, state that there is a healing, restoring power in the church that is productive of emotional health and wholeness. And indeed there is! But what to do?

Perhaps one of the first things to do is for us who are the church to admit honestly that the church has a problem, and has had a problem for a long time. We could begin by being a little less defensive and a little more open to the possibility that maybe the church could in fact be contributing to mental illness.

That could possibly be threatening. We know from experience that a heightening of awareness is sometimes scary. But the first step in the solution of any problem is the admission and acceptance of the problem. The church could then be on the way towards beginning to realize its great potential as a resource for the fostering of mental health and the prevention of mental ill-health. I have said before, it is no coincidence that there is such a close tie between a person's emotional life and his spiritual life. In the quotation at the beginning of this chapter Dr. Jung speaks vividly to this fact.

The majority of people who break down seem to manifest certain similar attitudes and behaviors.

1. For one reason or another they were generally afraid to express their real feelings.

2. They didn't have an opportunity to "talk through" their conflicts and stresses. They were unable to find a "listening ear."

3. The people with whom they *did* talk didn't really hear what they were saying.

4. They generally felt that sheer will power could overcome their problem, even though they really didn't understand it.

5. They denied reality and moved into their own world which was less painful, less confusing, less demanding and had fewer responsibilities to meet and decisions to make.

Now it seems clear that the church possesses the necessary "stuff" to help people deal with every one of those five areas so that they don't have to break down. But to employ the "stuff" requires changes—a change in emphasis, a change in attitude, a new openness, a new freedom. Perhaps even risk!

For instance, number one above speaks to the basic matter of the repression or expression of feelings. In response we as a church could give some consideration to that old axiom, "Express your feelings and you ride them. Repress your feelings and they ride you." People do in fact become ill because they are afraid to express their feelings, afraid that somehow it would be wrong or unchristian if they expressed grief or fear or anger or doubt or deep disappointment and other strong feelings. Truly we should be more afraid of what happens when we deny and bottle up these feelings rather than when we express them.

But there is both a propriety and an impropriety about expressing feelings. It is possible that the expression of feelings might be unhealthy as well as healthy, or destructive as well as constructive. In the chapter on feelings I made the association between expression of feelings and control. It is a fact that the occurrence of feelings within us is beyond our control. We will automatically have feelings just as automatically as we will feel hunger in the absence of food. But in *acting* on those feelings we can employ the concept of control very meaningfully. We may have no control over what we feel, but we certainly can control (we need to control) what we *do* about those feelings, how we act on them, how we express them.

I have come to think in terms of "impulsiveness" and "spontaneity" when describing expression of (or acting on) feelings. It seems that both concepts satisfy the need to express feelings but spontaneity possesses a control which is absent in impulsiveness. In spontaneous expression the person is more in charge of the feeling; in impulsive expression the feeling is more in the driver's seat. Impulsive behavior seems to bypass personal filters and governors almost completely, whereas spontaneous behavior, though free and uninhibited, is appropriate, primarily in that it does not hurt people. Impulsive behavior is simply more uncontrolled, more base. Impulsive people just "let fly" their feelings, positive and negative, with little or no regard for the surroundings of the situation. The impulsive person may shout out a joyful proclamation when the setting is totally inappropriate (begin to laugh raucously in a library reading room) or he may smash his fist into his child's head as he expresses his anger to his child. Generally speaking, impulsive expression of feelings (especially feelings of anger) is more destructive than constructive. Acting on feelings in one way or another may give a certain relief to a person, but if he hurts another person in the process it doesn't help him to feel better afterward.

Spontaneous expression of feelings, on the other hand, is also an authentic, genuine act, but it employs control by the refinements of propriety. I do not mean that the spontaneous person "runs his feelings through the computer" before he acts on them, but his expression of his feelings is so controlled that he does not hurt people. Yet he relieves the energy of the feeling by expressing it rather than denying it or suppressing it. His expression is healthy and constructive and may open or leave open the channels for communication.

The spontaneous expression of anger as opposed to an impulsive expression could be illustrated with a common problem between father and son. The young son leaves his bicycle in the middle of the garage when his father wants to drive the car in for the night. The father has asked his son two or three times to remember to park his bike elsewhere than in the middle of the garage, but the boy continues to leave it in the way. Finally in genuine anger the father confronts his son one night saying, "John, I am very angry with you because you continue to leave that bicycle right where I want to park the car, so that I have to stop the car, get out, move the bike, get back in and then drive the car in." The father has expressed his feeling, discharged the energy; his stance, his voice, his facial expression have been consistent with his words, and his son has gotten the message. The encounter has been healthy and constructive. If, however, the father acted on his feeling of anger impulsively rather than spontaneously, the would probably storm in the house, grab the boy, shake him, call him an irresponsible idiot, drag him into the garage and make him move the bike. That encounter would be unhealthy and destructive. But in both cases the man would have expressed his feelings.

If the situation occurred again (which is quite possible in both instances) the father acting spontaneously could express his anger by putting the bicycle in the trunk of his car and leaving it there for a few days. Undoubtedly his son would be more careful after that, at least for a while. The father acting impulsively on his feeling of anger might simply drive the car over the bicycle and crush it.

Like so many things, feelings themselves are innocent and neutral. It is how we act or do not act on them that determines whether the experience shall be constructive and healthy, or destructive and unhealthy.

We know instinctively that feelings are natural; but we need, in the church, an increased *awareness* of the naturalness of feelings within us. We need to learn that having feelings is okay. We need to learn that feelings can be expressed—need to be expressed—in an appropriate way. We need not fear feelings; we need only fear repressing them. We need encouragement to strive for congruence between our inner feelings and our outer expressions that we might be genuine and authentic people rather than phonies. Enough of the "laughing on the outside, crying on the inside" kind of deception. Enough of the "put on a happy face" kind of admonition. I have seen a man sitting at a table with me who was so angry his lips were pursed, the veins stood out on his neck, and his fists were clenched. Yet he could not even admit to the anger within himself, let alone express it. He could only speak acceptable pleasantries. I have talked with people before surgery who were so tight with anxiety they seemed ready to snap. But they could not allow the feeling to find expression. Instead they reported on the degree of their faith.

God in his wisdom made us to have feelings, so that it is not so much a matter of learning how to express them as it is a matter of ceasing to put the damper on their natural expression. We *can* express feelings, if only we can *let* ourselves express them. We don't have to deny them, keep them inside, become artificial and defensive (because of our insecurity), and work ourselves into a breakdown. There is of course always some risk involved in expressing feelings appropriately; but I would hope that by now we would be able to realize that the greater risk truly lies in *not* expressing them.

If we can move in the direction of becoming able

to feel more free in expressing our true feelings in human relationships, perhaps we can also feel freer to express our real feelings to God. That really is what prayer is about. And you certainly find no lack of such a pouring out in biblical personalities. God, you know, isn't so weak that he would be wiped out if you got mad at him and expressed your feelings. You know that many times you do get mad at him even if you don't admit it. And he knows it anyway, so you might as well express it and quit carrying around the emotional charge of it, adding to all your other repressions and suppressions. I had an experience once with an old man—a terminal patient—who one day finally gave vent to his feelings toward God and laid out all the "baggage" he had been carrying inside for longer than he could remember. His tears of anger were hot, but they were healthy. He said that never in his life had he felt so close to God and never before had he felt so vividly the overwhelming acceptance that wrapped itself around him. And he said he knew that God really is love.

Let the church encourage and promote and nourish and say "yes" to authentic, transparent prayer that opens a person's inner self through the expression of his feelings. Authentic expression of feelings through prayers in worship services encourages people to be more free and expressive in their private prayer.

Concerning worship and feelings, one very positive

element evident in parts of the church is the growing renewal and revitalization of liturgy and worship. There is much excitement and creativity going into contemporizing worship experiences. Respectability, it seems, does not really have to be idolized after all. Joy and celebration are increasingly reflected. Let it be! For too long the church has been dour. Let authentic feelings of happiness and exuberance regain their rightful place in religious experience.

Another major area where we can do something in the church is the area of acceptance, acceptance of self and of others. Perhaps a revision of Christian anthropology on the grass roots level would be in order. Can the church help people to become more aware of themselves? I believe so. If acceptance is to be realized, awareness needs to precede it. And the church definitely has the resources to help people to awareness and acceptance of themselves.

For instance, we can begin by laying aside some of those unreasonable expectations which legalism and piety and rigidity in the church have demanded. We often tend to take ourselves much too seriously. We can, instead, let humor and laughter happen. We can become able to laugh at ourselves. We can relax the compulsion to be behaviorally perfect. Not to the point of irresponsibility or license, certainly, but to the truly human level. We can stop neglecting the earthiness of ourselves. We can accept our shadow side, become acquainted with it, not be afraid of it or deny it. We are *not* always good, and that is a fact; but that does not mean that God ceases to love us.

This reminds me of the misleading benediction which the church school teacher innocently gave to her class as they departed one Sunday morning: "Now be good, children, so God will love you."

We have trouble learning to live with our shadow side, our dark side, our not-so-good side, even though it is truly a part of our humanity. So it takes courage to admit it, to say yes to it, to say "It is I." But when it happens and a person can "embrace" his shadow the need for many of his masks fades away. He may allow himself to be authentic and genuine. The expectations for performance of unreasonable feats of faith and behavior do not have to be. A person can "be himself."

This is not especially easy. If there is one common cry that seems to rise up from people in emotional distress it is: "I am a human being; but oh how hard it is sometimes to accept my humanity! I am myself and can only be me; but how hard it is sometimes to be myself!"

So let the church teach appropriate love of self—that is the basis, the foundation of self-acceptance according to Jesus. If *God* loves and accepts me as I am, certainly I can love and accept myself. This love and acceptance can then move to others—spouse, children, friends, and neighbors. It can be more comfortable to accept others in their humanity too; to see the individuality and uniqueness of persons. Knowing and accepting my own imperfection goes a long way in accepting the imperfection of my fellows.

Perhaps this would also enable us to be more sensitive to what others are saying and to respond with a part of ourselves. How clearly this speaks to the second and third common observations of people who break down: They didn't have an opportunity to "talk through" their conflicts and stresses (they were unable to find a "listening ear") and, the people with whom they *did* talk didn't really hear what they were saying.

Can the church provide listening ears? It would *seem* that we in the church should be able to provide listening ears as well as, if not better than, anyone else. After all, we say we care. We can certainly become more sensitive to what others (spouse, children especially) are *really* saying—that is, hearing their *feelings* behind their words. Of course that takes time and effort. And we can respond to them with a part of ourselves—invest something of *our* feelings into them. We might be able to become authentic and genuine in the relationship. We might be able to give a non-possessive warmth that can be felt. We might be able to begin to move in the direction of becoming truly empathic people. If we can move in the direction of learning the ministry of *being,* hopefully we can relax the compulsion of always having to *do* something. That is not to say that doing does not have its place; but it *is* to say that *being* generally has been neglected in relationships, because doing is really easier and less risky. A colleague once told me that his instruction to people who are more concerned with doing than being is, "Don't just do something; stand there!"

If it is indeed true that the main cause of breakdown lies in some serious malfunction of a person's experience of love, then the most productive atmosphere for healing should be the human relationship wherein authentic love can be *felt* in terms of acceptance, empathy, compassion, warmth, and genuineness.

Another thing we can do in the church is encourage more positive self images. The emphasis could be shifted, and we could begin to see anew how strongly the whole message of Christianity stresses the worth and value of man and woman.

"In human experience it is a rare thing for one man to give his life for another, even if the latter be a good man, though there have been a few who have had the courage to do it. Yet the proof of God's amazing love is this: that it was *while we were sinners* that Christ died for us. Moreover if he did that for us while we were sinners, now that we are men justified by the shedding of his blood, what reason have we to fear the wrath of God? If, while we were his enemies, Christ reconciled us to God by *dying for us,* surely now that we are reconciled we may be perfectly certain of our salvation through his *living in us.*" (Romans 5:6-11; Phillips).

How much more clearly than this could God express

the good news which is the foundation of the church and the key to man's wholeness? Through Jesus he has shown us and proved to us his acceptance of us as we are. Through Jesus we come into a reconciling relationship with God which he will never withdraw. Therefore it is obvious that our value and worth is tremendous, and we can justifiably and with good conscience have a high and healthy self-image. We can be self-accepting, affirming our strengths and acknowledging our weakness. We can with joy and assurance calmly say, "I am justified. I am reconciled. God loves me."

Rather than worrying about people becoming proud and arrogant, perhaps we should be more concerned how self-debasement in the name of religion can cripple a person for life. Rather than beating down pride, perhaps we can teach and live humility. And here again self-acceptance figures prominently. True humility rests on self-acceptance. False humility rests on self-rejection. False humility is to deny one's true assets. False humility is for a beautiful woman to consider herself "homely"; it is for a brilliant man to consider himself a dunce. False humility is to say, "Oh it was nothing," when you know full well your performance was magnificent.

True humility is to accept fully and be deeply grateful for your talents, gifts, achievements, and successes. True humility is to be free to rejoice in your own tal-

ents and accomplishments just as frankly and as grate-
fully as you rejoice in the talents and accomplishments
of others.

It would help, too, if we took a new look at the man,
Jesus Christ, as he walks through the gospels, and not
as many have painted him. He can help us in our self
image as we learn to identify with him as a person
who knew and accepted his humanity and never
wanted to deny it, as a man who himself knew the
whole gamut of feelings, as a human being who
touched the hearts of other human beings because he
accepted *their* humanity.

One of the richest sources for meeting the human,
earthy Jesus is Clarence Jordan's, *Cotton Patch Version
of the New Testament.* When you see him walking
through those pages you thrill, like perhaps never before, at identifying with this Jesus—the Son of man.

There is truly a well of strength in the church, because the strength of Almighty God can be channeled
through it. That is not to say that the strength of Almighty God cannot be found outside the church; it
definitely can. But the church can direct people to its
source of strength, and help those persons accept it.
With the availability of that kind of strength, it is
easier to face realistically the often rugged problems
of life. Perhaps with that strength a person doesn't
have to run from reality.

What a tremendous resource the church *can* be in

helping people to understand fully their relationships to themselves, to their fellows, and to God. What a freeing, releasing agent it *can* be, giving the joy of spiritual and emotional health. "After all," said Jesus, "don't forget that the reason why I came was that you might have life—and have it to its fullest!"